STAYING HOME

By Elaine W. Rifkin

[BAY to SHORE Discoveries]

© 2009 by Elaine W. Rifkin

Book Design by Kristine G. Rifkin • Baltimore, MD

Photography and Journal Entries from 2003–2009

Library of Congress Cataloging in Publication Data

Rifkin, Elaine W.
  Staying Home: Bay to Shore Discoveries / by Elaine W. Rifkin
  ISBN – 13: 978-0-615-29623-4
  ISBN – 10: 0-615-29623-8
  Library of Congress Control Number: 2009905383

First Edition

Regent Publishing Services, Ltd. Hong Kong

Printed in China on Acid-Free Paper

6:48 am The rising sun kisses the horizon.

FOREWORD

Like many kids, I played Little League baseball. From the pitcher's mound, I could toss a fastball with the best of them. I was no Nolan Ryan, but I did strike out 17 batters once (there are only 18 outs in a Little League game)! I was even voted to the league All-Star team in my final year of play. It was a thrill and an honor to be a part of such a special group of players. But by the start of the second All-Star practice, I was no longer a member of the team.

Earlier in the day, I had phoned the coach to tell him that I had decided to quit. Believe me…It was a difficult phone call for a 13 year-old ballplayer to initiate. To make matters worse, the coach let me know in no uncertain terms that he was angry. He just didn't seem to understand that my heart and interests were elsewhere. How could he? Despite his best efforts to command a change in my decision, I was steadfast in my resolve to keep the rest of my summer weekends free and clear. Remaining on the team meant that I would be sacrificing opportunities to fish, crab, clam and marsh-muck during weekends spent at our family's summer residence near Rehoboth Bay. That was just way too much to ask!

Such is the allure of Delaware's Inland Bays! The laugh of a gull; a cool ocean breeze; a fat blue crab tangled in a dip net; the rise and fall of the tide. Each is a gesture that beckons to us. And, we respond en masse. Millions of visitors flock to the area each year, much like the Native Americans who used to spend the warmer months camped near the bays' plentiful waters. Unfortunately, much has changed since the days when the Nanticoke tribe enjoyed the bounty of these bays. Our Inland Bays have been in peril for years and continue to suffer from poor water quality and habitat loss.

Staying Home invites you to experience the splendor and beauty of the Inland Bays estuary from a unique perspective. From the confines of her property on Little Assawoman Bay, Elaine Rifkin has masterfully captured in her photos the natural treasures of this area. It is my hope that Elaine's gift to all of us inspires you to recognize the rich natural history of our "estuary of national importance" and act to preserve and protect Delaware's Inland Bays, unique gems in the Diamond State.

Edward A. Lewandowski
Executive Director, Delaware Center for the Inland Bays • May, 2009
www.inlandbays.org

TO ERIK

Always there

" We live on a narrow stretch of land between Little Assawoman Bay and the Atlantic Ocean affording spectacular views of wildlife in natural wetland and shore habitats. These photographs taken over many years illustrate the diversity of life here, offering hope to all who strive to protect and maintain these precious resources.

The notion of StayingHOME refers literally to capturing images within the discrete area of our property lines. It also gently suggests taking the time to notice and to have a stake in one's surroundings.

The book spans one day—sunrise to sunset—with journal entries accompanying the photographs.

Enjoy. " — EWR/2009 • www.stayingHOMEphotog.com

6:50 am   STRANGE BEDFELLOWS

The coat of the red fox is darker in mid May lending contrast to the pure white of the snowy egrets in this unusual grouping.

7:01 am | SUNLIT GREAT BLUE HERONS

Six sleeping side by side in the Inland Pond, or perhaps they are sheltering from the cold and wind of this Easter morning.

7:20 am | TAGGED SANDERLING

The lime green tag and letters indicate a Delaware Bay bird most likely tagged during spring shorebird monitoring.

7:30 am | BREAKFAST CLUB | >

On September mornings, gulls, egrets, herons and terns gather in great numbers to feed noisily in the inland ponds.

Here egrets and gulls predominate.

7:38 am   K N E E   D E E P

This solitary immature green heron waits motionless among the *Spartina* for prey to appear.

7:39 am | MIRROR IMAGE

On this cool, clear June morning, a snowy egret feeds in the Inland Pond, its bill piercing its reflection.

7:39 am DEER ON TERN ISLAND >

Surprisingly, a doe from the wildlife refuge spends several minutes on this small island before swimming home.

7:46 am

7:40 am   FLEDGLING OSPREYS

By the third week of July, the new ospreys can fly. Within the next couple of months, they will learn the skills needed for their long migration south.

7:41 am | PRECARIOUS PERCH | >

A mallard poses handsomely on a clod in the Waterway, all of his bright colors reflecting late April morning sun.

7:45 am | TERRITORIAL IMPERATIVE

Ospreys return to their nesting places from South America each mid March, and almost immediately begin nest building.

They have little tolerance for interlopers and fiercely defend their territory.

7:55 am MUSKRAT HEAVEN >

This industrious mammal, oblivious to the great egret on the bank, swims all around the waterways collecting *Phragmites* and long stemmed daisies for its lair.

7:58 am | PERFECT CAMOUFLAGE

The red fox is picking its way through the late March wetland grasses; the early sun illuminating its beautiful searching eyes.

8:14 am | CURIOUS VISITOR | >

A male grackle stares from atop the hollywood juniper; yellow eyes, lustrous blue-black plumage and wedge tail all visible.

8:21 am | FORSTER'S TERN IN FLIGHT | >

They are everywhere this late April morning, squabbling with each other in between diving for fish.

8:24 am | SNOWY EGRETS

On this cold and sunny April morning, flocks of "snowys," luminous in this light, fly north into the forty mile per hour wind gusts.

8:28 am | NORTH AMERICAN RIVER OTTER

A distinct trail in the Inlet announces the arrival of a playful otter with its flat head, ears on the sides and broad hairless nose.

Otters feast on crabs and their presence is a hopeful sign of the health of the bay.

| 8:30 am | LITTLE BLUE HERONS | > |

A pair of these rare herons lands briefly in the Inland Pond to wade together before flying off.

8:43 am | WILD TURKEY | >

She meanders through the brown wetlands gobbling softly, iridescent plumage visible through the stalks.

8:57 am — RED-BREASTED MERGANSERS

A resplendent male and his mate with black encircled eyes make a jaunty couple this March day.

9:00 am | FLYING SOLO

Brown pelicans arrived on Delmarva more than 20 years ago and now are a common sight over beach and bays.

9:06 am | CANADA GOOSE

A solitary goose settles into the wetland grasses showing off its unique coloration and grand size.

9:10 am | GLOSSY IBISES

Many flocks of ibises fly over the bays, but this April morning one group flies over the wetlands, allowing a close look at their green and brown plumage.

9:28 am GREAT BLUE HERON >

Some herons are more adept than others at catching fish but two at once requires skill at hanging on to them.

The heron waits patiently for the fish to tire and manages to eat them both.

9:30 am | OSPREY WITH FISH

This fledgling, born about four months ago, has mastered the difficult task of catching a fish in the ocean and bringing it bayside to eat.

9:43 am   CROWNS ALOFT

A snowy egret and tricolor heron challenge each other by the pond's edge; the tricolor flies off.

9:48 am   L U N A   M O T H

This nocturnal moth hangs from a stella d'oro plant, closed wings signifying it is at rest.

When frightened, it exposes its four "wing eyes" to appear more ominous.

10:02 am | BUSH KATYDID

August insects riotous with color; this one poses on a closed hibiscus bloom.

10:16 am | TRICOLOR HERONS | >

A pair feeds together in the Inland Pond, a very rare sight on Little Assawoman Bay.

It is easy to see why some think of them as the most beautiful heron.

10:47 am | SWIRLING FISH

Schools of little fish in the Inlet—sustenance for the waders and shore birds—are catching food of their own.

11:00 am   "THIN AS A RAIL"   >

A family of two adult and six black chicks crosses the Inland Pond at low tide this August day.

With narrow bodies and long toes, clapper rails are well adapted to this wetland environment.

11:00 am | NOVEMBER SNOW GEESE | >

They fill the sky over Little Assawoman Wildlife Refuge, a lone pine seen through the mist.

11:10 am GRAY HAIRSTREAK

The proboscis of the tiny butterfly is taking in nectar from the tube-like extensions of the saltmarsh fleabane.

11:12 am DINING MUSKRAT

A meal of *Phragmites* is delicately held with long nails.

11:16 am | ROLE MODELING

This May day, the duck is teaching her ducklings to forage in the mud of low tide; they line up to follow her lead.

11:26 am | MATING GRASSHOPPERS

Females deposit up to eight egg masses each with about 25 eggs into soil near weeds.

In spring, nymphs hatch, molt several times and in two months or so, look just like adults.

11:38 am | BLACK SNAKES >

Black birds are calling warnings about several five to six foot snakes warming themselves in the Bayberry Stand.

Late March, they are just out of hibernation and two months later they are mating in the same area.

11:40 am | GREAT EGRET WITH FISH | >

Occurring in a split second, the capture at the surface reveals the interaction between bird and prey.

11:53 am   ELEGANT CRAB SPIDER   >

In the dunes a tiny spider, which changes color to match its environs, has captured a skipper moth.

The grains of sand look like little pebbles.

12:08 pm | MALE AMERICAN GOLDFINCH

Late summer is the breeding season for this species and they are courting as they zip in and out of the wildflowers.

A male settles in with three black-eyed susan blossoms and delicately extracts seeds.

12:22 pm | BUSY BEE | >

The bumble bee in the verbena has symmetrical globs of pollen on its hind legs.

Bees will travel 15 mph visiting 50 to 1,000 flowers a day collecting nectar and pollen.

12:33 pm — EYES OF BIRD AND PREY

At midday, surrounded by *Spartina* in the rippling Waterway, a great egret lunches on a small fish.

12:50 pm | BIG CATCH | >

A great blue heron, spearing a flounder with its top bill, moves to the Inlet bank.

After carefully maneuvering the fish into its throat, this magnificent bird swallows it down.

1:00 pm

1:14 pm GREEN HERON

Searching for prey along the Inlet bank this adult, with its blue-green plumage and orange legs, looks quite different from the brown streaked juvenile.

1:53 pm   FEMALE SEASIDE DRAGONLET   >

Dragonflies have compact touching eyes and differently shaped fore and hind wings held 180° to their body at rest.

When approached gently, they tolerate human presence.

2:19 pm | DIAMONDBACK TERRAPINS | >

Early June, the terrapins are courting in the Inlet with the smaller male pursuing the much larger female.

They reproduce after eight years of age and dig six inch nests to lay their white to pink eggs, which hatch between 60 to 120 days.

2:53 pm THE CHASE

Looking fearsome with spread wings, extended neck and bill in the air, the great blue heron chases the great egret out of the Inlet.

3:10 pm | TRICOLOR HERON IN PINE | >

The red-brown feathers of this immature heron stand out among the dark green needles of the pine tree.

4:00 pm | MANTID IN DUNES | >

The praying mantis, well camouflaged in the seaside goldenrod, waits for a monarch butterfly to land nearby this October afternoon.

INDIGENOUS MARSH MALLOWS

7:46 pm Sunset.